MW00876977

The Little Book of
PLANES

by Billy Steers

Random House 🏠 New York

Copyright © 2000 by Billy Steers. All rights reserved under International and Pan-American Copyright Conventions. Published in the United States by Random House, Inc., New York, and simultaneously in Canada by Random House of Canada Limited, Toronto.
Library of Congress Cataloging-in-Publication Data Steers, Billy. The little book of planes / by Billy Steers. p. cm. — (Jellybean books) Summary: Illustrations and simple text present a variety of different types of aircraft, including a cargo transport, crop duster, Harrier, seaplane, and more. ISBN 0-375-80219-3
1. Airplanes—Juvenile literature. [1. Airplanes.] I. Title. II. Series. TL547.S794 2000 387.7'3—dc21 98-53287
www.randomhouse.com/kids
Printed in the United States of America January 2000 10 9 8 7 6 5 4 3 2 1
JELLYBEAN BOOKS, RANDOM HOUSE, and the Random House colophon are registered trademarks and the Jellybean Books colophon is a trademark of Random House, Inc.

Let Wembley Gremlin tell you all about airplanes!

Airplanes start out as a bunch of parts and are put together in big factories.

The wings, the tail, and the engines
are connected to the body.

The plane goes through lots of safety checks before it can carry people.

Look at all the screens, buttons, and levers in the cockpit!

Airplanes need runways to take off from and land on. The control tower directs the pilots.

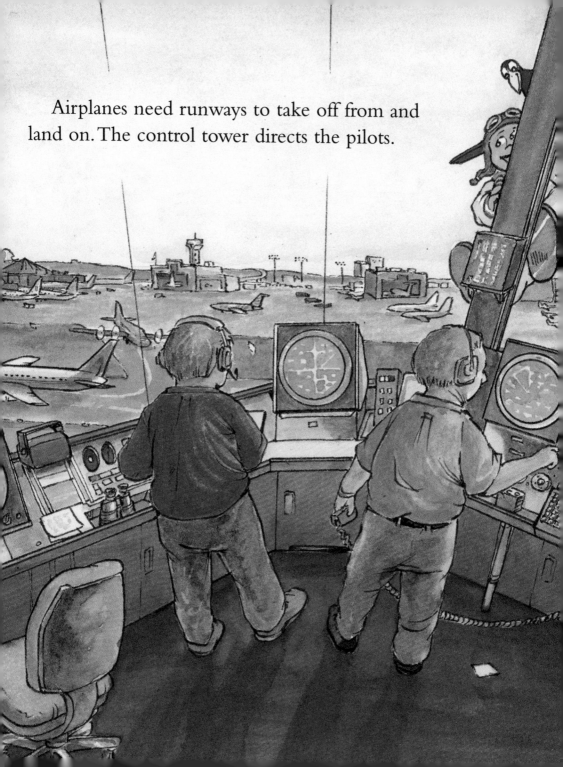

Many different types of airplanes share
the runway at busy airports.

Helicopters and a type of jet called a "Harrier"
take off straight up and can land anywhere.

The Gulfstream is a business jet.
"I'm off to my meeting."

Fighter planes are built for speed.
"Cleared for takeoff."

There are very small one-person aircraft and
huge cargo transports—like the C-5 Galaxy.
    "Say ahh…"

Here's what one cargo plane looks like inside.
I cut it in half to show you!

Airplanes do so many things.
Some airplanes are "crop dusters"
and work on the farm.

Some rescue people
at sea. "Hooray!"

Planes are used
to spot traffic jams

and fight forest fires.

Pilots normally avoid
bad weather, but this plane
goes right into hurricanes
to study them!

Seaplanes land on water, and
skiplanes land on snow.
  "*Brr!* It's cold in the Arctic!"

I like planes that do tricks…

...and old planes that still fly.

When planes have flown their last flight, they go to the "boneyard" in the desert for storage,

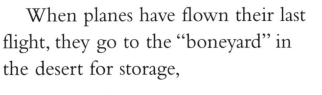

or they go to a museum for all to enjoy.

Planes old and new are always fun to see!